MY NEW PET

MY PET DOG

BY NANCY GREENWOOD

Gareth Stevens Publishing

Please visit our website, www.garethstevens.com. For a free color catalog of all our high-quality books, call toll free 1-800-542-2595 or fax 1-877-542-2596.

Portions of this work were originally authored by Cecelia H. Brannon and published as *Pet Dogs.* All new material this edition authored by Nancy Greenwood.

Library of Congress Cataloging-in-Publication Data
Names: Greenwood, Nancy, author.
Title: My pet dog / Nancy Greenwood.
Description: New York : Gareth Stevens Publishing, [2023] | Series: My new pet | Includes index.
Identifiers: LCCN 2021061107 | ISBN 9781538280966 (set) | ISBN 9781538280973 (library binding) | ISBN 9781538280959 (paperback) | ISBN 9781538280980 (ebook)
Subjects: LCSH: Dogs–Juvenile literature.
Classification: LCC SF426.5 .G74 2023 | DDC 636.7–dc23/eng/20220111
LC record available at https://lccn.loc.gov/2021061107

Published in 2023 by
Gareth Stevens Publishing
29 East 21st Street
New York, NY 10010

Designer: Andrea Davison-Bartolotta
Editor: Kristen Nelson

Photo credits: Cover, p.1 Miguel Valente/Shutterstock.com; series art (backgrounds) Magnia/Shutterstock.com; p. 5 BIGANDT.COM/Shutterstock.com; p. 7 Rita_Kochmarjova/Shutterstock.com; p. 9 LightField Studios/Shutterstock.com; p. 11 FamVeld/Shutterstock.com; p. 13 anetapics/Shutterstock.com; p. 15 Pixel-Shot/Shutterstock.com; p. 17 New Africa/Shutterstock.com; p. 19 Serget Fatin/Shutterstock.com; p. 21 Ormalternative/Shutterstock.com.

Printed in the United States of America

CPSIA compliance information: Batch #CSGS23: For further information contact Gareth Stevens, New York, New York at 1-800-542-2595.

CONTENTS

Boldface words appear in the glossary.

Your Pet Dog

Having a pet can be fun! It is also a big **responsibility**. If you want a pet that is friendly and always happy to see you, a dog may be a good **choice**. Read on to see why dogs make great pets!

Puppy Time!

When dogs are born, they're called puppies. Puppies are much smaller than their parents. But they will soon be just as big! Young puppies get food from their mother's milk. If that's not available, they can be fed special food.

Having any dog is a lot of work. Puppies can be even more work because they are still learning things like where to go to the bathroom and how to behave, or act. If you've never had a pet, you may want to **adopt** an adult dog.

All About Dogs

A dog has a wet nose. It can smell things people cannot smell. A dog's fur is called a coat. The coat keeps dogs warm and makes them soft to pet. Dogs like to be pet, but remember to be gentle!

Playtime!

Dogs love to play! They have lots of **energy**. There are many kinds of toys you can get your dog. They can also learn tricks. They can roll over, raise their paws, and **fetch**. Dogs like to go for walks with their owner too.

Doggie Down Time

Dogs like to chew on bones. This helps keep their teeth clean. When they're not playing or eating, dogs can sleep a lot. They can dream and even **snore**! Make sure you have a nice place for your dog to sleep.

Keeping Your Dog Healthy

Dogs need to go to the doctor just like you! A dog's doctor is called a **veterinarian**, or vet. Healthy dogs should go see the vet once a year. The veterinarian can also help if your dog ever gets sick.

Time to Eat!

Dogs eat and drink water from bowls. Your veterinarian can help you learn what kind of food is best for your dog. This is commonly some kind of **kibble**. Dogs should not eat what you eat. Some people food can be bad for them.

Loving Your Dog

If you get a dog, you are in charge of caring for it. Most dogs love being around their owners. Some will even follow you around. Dogs need food, water, a cozy place to sleep—and lots of love!

GLOSSARY

adopt: To make part of a family.

choice: A pick between two or more possibilities.

energy: The ability to be active.

fetch: To go after and bring back an object, such as a ball.

kibble: Ground meal or grain often shaped into pellets and used for animal food.

responsibility: Something a person is in charge of.

snore: To breathe noisily while sleeping.

veterinarian: A doctor who is trained to treat animals.

FOR MORE INFORMATION

BOOKS

Jaycox, Jaclyn. *Read All About Dogs.* North Mankato, MN: Pebble, 2021.

Titmus, Dawn. *Dogs.* New York, NY: PowerKids Press, 2019.

Vink, Amanda. *Is a Dog a Good Pet for Me?* New York, NY: PowerKids Press, 2020.

WEBSITES

Dogs
www.ducksters.com/animals/dogs.php
Read more about different kinds of dogs on this website.

Domestic Dogs
www.dkfindout.com/us/animals-and-nature/dogs/domestic-dogs/
Learn all about domestic, or pet, dogs on this interactive page.

Publisher's note to educators and parents: Our editors have carefully reviewed these websites to ensure that they are suitable for students. Many websites change frequently, however, and we cannot guarantee that a site's future contents will continue to meet our high standards of quality and educational value. Be advised that students should be closely supervised whenever they access the internet.

INDEX